Dr. Seuss
We Love You

Patricia Stone Martin

illustrated by Karen Park

Rourke Enterprises   Vero Beach, Florida

©1987 by Rourke Enterprises, Inc.

Manufactured in the United States of America

Library of Congress Cataloging-in-Publication Data

Martin, Patricia Stone.
  Dr. Seuss – we love you.

  (Reaching your goal biographies)
  Summary: A brief biography of Theodor Geisel who, under the name Dr. Seuss, gained fame as an author and illustrator of books for children. Includes advice on setting and reaching goals.
  1. Seuss, Dr. – Biography – Juvenile literature. 2. Authors, American – 20th century – Biography – Juvenile literature. 3. Illustrators – United States – Biography – Juvenile literature. 4. Children's literature – Authorship – Juvenile literature. [1. Seuss, Dr. 2. Authors, American. 3. Illustrators] I. Title. II. Series: Martin, Patricia Stone. Reaching your goal biographies.
PS3513.E2Z78 1987 813'.52 [B] [92] 87-12920
ISBN 0-86592-168-7

Theodor Geisel made some marks on his schoolbook. He looked at his book. He could not help smiling. He had drawn some funny people and animals. Theodor loved to draw on his books. He thought of animals that no one had ever seen. He practiced drawing them on his books. They made him happy.

Today Theodor Geisel's drawings and stories make many people happy. Now when he writes and draws he uses another name. He uses the name Dr. Seuss.

Theodor Seuss Geisel was born in Springfield, Massachusetts, on March 2, 1904. He had a sister named Margaretta.

Theodor graduated from high school in Springfield. Then he went to Dartmouth College in Hanover, New Hampshire. He wrote and drew cartoons for the college magazine.

In 1925, he went to Oxford University in England. He met Helen Palmer while he was there. Theodor did not stay at Oxford. Instead he traveled in Europe.

Theodor and Helen were married in 1927. When they came back to the United States, Theodor drew cartoons. He sold them to magazines. Then he did artwork for advertisements.

Theodor decided he wanted to write and illustrate children's books. The first book he wrote and illustrated was an alphabet book. No one published it. He did not write another book for four years.

In 1936, Theodor went to Europe again. On the way back, he sat on the deck of the ship. The ship's engines seemed to be talking to him. "Ta-da, ta-da, ta-da," sang the engines. Theodor listened. "Ta-da, ta-da, ta-da."

Slowly, the words to a story came into Theodor's mind. They fit the sounds the engines were making. The story told what a little boy saw on Mulberry Street. At first all the boy saw was a horse and a wagon. Then more and more things came to his mind — funny things like a reindeer pulling a sleigh.

An elephant pulling a band came into view. Police began to lead them. The mayor cheered them. Finally, an airplane flew over and dropped bright bits of paper. More and more people joined the parade. But all the little boy had really seen on Mulberry Street was a plain horse and a wagon.

Theodor wrote down the words to this story. He made bright pictures to go with it. He named the story *And to Think That I Saw It on Mulberry Street*. The book was published and was a big success. Almost fifty years later, it is still one of most children's favorite books.

That was Dr. Seuss's first published book. Theodor had decided to use that name when he wrote for children. Seuss was his mother's last name before she was married. Theodor was not really a doctor!

In 1939, another book by Dr. Seuss was published. It was a story called *The King's Stilts*. Since then, many more books by Dr. Seuss have been published.

During World War II, Theodor was in the army. He wrote for his country. He did not use the name Dr. Seuss then. One film he wrote won an Academy Award in 1946. He won other awards for his films too.

In 1948, Helen and Theodor moved to a lovely house on top of a mountain in La Jolla, California. They could see the ocean from their home. Theodor like to look at the ocean while he wrote.

After the war Theodor went back to being Dr. Seuss. He wrote and illustrated many stories. Most of his books are written in verse.

Some of Dr. Seuss's books teach a lesson. In *Yertle the Turtle*, Dr. Seuss says that everyone should be free. In *Gertrude McFuzz*, he is saying that we should be happy with what we have. In *Horton Hears a Who*, he says that even the smallest person can help.

His stories are filled with strange animals and people. Readers never know what they will see next. It might be a Stroodel or a Twiddler Owl. It might be a Yook or a Zook. It might even be a Zin-a-zu Bird or a Tizzle-Topped Grouse.

17

In 1957, *The Cat in the Hat* was published. It was a book for first-grade readers. Dr. Seuss knew that boys and girls would like reading if they had books that were fun to read.

Theodor and Helen started Beginner Books in 1958. Beginner Books are easy to read. The books are also fun to read. Dr. Seuss writes some of these books. When he does not draw the pictures himself, he uses the name Theo LeSieg. (LeSieg is Geisel spelled backwards!) Other people also write and illustrate Beginner Books.

Helen Geisel died in 1967. Theodor married Audry Diamond the next year. They still live on the same mountaintop where they can see the ocean. And Dr. Seuss is still writing stories for boys and girls.

In 1986, Dr. Seuss wrote a different kind of book. It is not for boys and girls. It is not even for their parents. It is for their grandparents. It is called *You're Only Old Once!* Now older people have their very own Dr. Seuss book.

Theodor Geisel had a goal. He wanted to write books that were easy to read. He also wanted to make reading fun. He reached his goal. Everyone has fun reading a Dr. Seuss book. Isn't it nice to know that you will never be too old to read a Dr. Seuss book?

Reaching Your Goal

What are your goals? Here are some steps
to help you reach them.

1. **Decide on your goal.**
   It may be a short-term goal like one
   of these:
   learning to ride a bike
   getting a good grade on a test
   keeping your room clean
   It may be a long-term goal like one
   of these:
   learning to read
   learning to play the piano
   becoming a lawyer

2. **Decide if your goal is something you
   really can do.**
   Do you have the talent you need?
   How can you find out? By trying!
   Will you need special equipment?
   Perhaps you need a piano or ice skates.
   How can you get what you need?
   Ask your teacher or your parents.

3. Decide on the first thing you must do.
Perhaps this will be to take lessons.

4. Decide on the second thing you must do.
Perhaps this will be to practice every day.

5. Start right away.
Stick to your plan until you reach your goal.

6. Keep telling yourself, "I can do it!"

Good luck! Maybe some day you will create new and funny books like Theodor Geisel.

Reaching Your Goal Books

Beverly Cleary
She Makes Reading Fun

Bill Cosby Superstar

Jesse Jackson A Rainbow Leader

Ted Kennedy, Jr.
A Lifetime of Challenges

Christa McAuliffe
Reaching for the Stars

Dale Murphy
Baseball's Gentle Giant

Dr. Seuss We Love You

Samantha Smith Young Ambassador

Rourke Enterprises, Inc.
P.O. Box 3328
Vero Beach, FL 32964